THE CYCLES OF NICHOLAS

A memoir of raising a child with
Fetal Alcohol Syndrome Disorder

INSPIRED

BALBOA
PRESS
A DIVISION OF HAY HOUSE

Balboa Press books may be ordered through booksellers or by contacting:

Balboa Press
A Division of Hay House
1663 Liberty Drive
Bloomington, IN 47403
www.balboapress.com
1 (877) 407-4847

Print information available on the last page.

ISBN: 978-1-9822-3145-3 (sc)
ISBN: 978-1-9822-3144-6 (hc)
ISBN: 978-1-9822-3151-4 (e)

Library of Congress Control Number: 2019909825

Balboa Press rev. date: 07/18/2019

This book is dedicated to all those that have lost their loved ones to the horrors of addiction.

CONTENTS

FOREWORD

I am privileged to consider the writer of this work one of my closest friends. Our relationship began twenty-eight years ago when we first met at the preschool attended by our young children. Our friendship as women blossomed as well as our friendship as married couples. I witnessed first hand the writer's struggles with infertility, a difficult marriage, and an amazingly hopeful adoption. Additionally, I witnessed fifteen years of fear, heartbreak, conflict, confusion, despair, and doubt. Finally, I witnessed faith, hope, enduring love, patience and commitment. As a friend and confident, I know, in my desire to help, I tried to impart my own advice and wisdom as the struggles with Nicholas moved from one desperate stage to the next. The truth is, I knew nothing. Yes, I experienced parenting ups and downs with my own children. But mine paled in comparison to what my friend was enduring. I could sympathize, but I couldn't empathize. I never actually walked in her shoes.

I am not unscarred by the illness of addiction as it has impacted my life in a very personal way. How many years did it take for me to trust the addict that I loved? Is it ever really possible, on the deepest level, to trust an addict again? What makes Nicholas' story so complicated is that his addiction was the manifestation of the biological damage done to him by his mother who drank alcohol while pregnant, then abandoned him to a state institution. Was there one doctor in all the years of treatment who clearly knew how to help this boy? No. Was there one medication that was found to be the perfect magic pill to help this boy? No. The one constant in all these years was my friend's unwavering commitment to help her son. I know there were moments of despair so dark that thoughts of giving him away or sending him back to Russia floated through her mind. But she persevered. I do not lie when I say that many of us believed we would be attending the funeral of this young addict - as we had attended others. There were days, weeks and months when I was afraid to ask "How is Nick doing?" because I believed the answer would make me flinch. However, the last time I asked that question, my heart was filled with hope. Could he be finally be winning the war or is it just another battle? Though I know addicts never completely conquer the monster that is drugs I pray he becomes stronger, more resilient and more confident so that when faced with the Monster again, he can walk away.

The significance of my friend's writing lies in the hope it may give to others who are walking, or have walked in her shoes. No one can predict Nick's future but we can pray that each new day finds him happy, healthy, stronger, and drug free.

J.M.

PREFACE

I procrastinated with the writing of this book; forever it seems. I have wrestled with sorting out my protestations, realizing that the writing of this book was as painful as it was to live through it. As I wrote each word I relived each moment. Fortunately, I had a nagging voice screaming in my head "Write the book!" If one woman doesn't drink during her pregnancy a life has been saved. If social services and social security would recognizes the impact of Fetal Alcohol Syndrome on families, schools, the courts, the incarcerated, medical insurance companies and society perhaps the services will become more readily available. If one person realizes the impact that addiction has on our global society than my message was heard. We all pay for the sins of our brothers and sisters! There is an urgent shortage of FASD communities in the United States.

This is a memoir of my years raising my son who was diagnosed with Fetal Alcohol Syndrome Disorder. I have changed the names to protect the privacy of everyone involved in this story. I ensure that every aspect of my story is true and that any misrepresentations were unintentional. The events and details are original. Yes, I really did live to talk about it. I purposely left out details about my other child and my ex husband. This is my journey in raising Nicholas, the beautiful 5 year old boy that I traveled the globe to adopt. Nicholas has a loving heart and is a good soul. He is sensitive, funny and thoughtful. He is a victim of alcohol abuse. His lifelong challenges are the manifestations bestowed upon him due to abuse of alcohol. Nicholas has much pain and shame in his life. I am sure that his biological mother shares the pain in her sober moments. It is a devastating disease.

This is my story of my perseverance in attempting to give him a better quality of life. It's also my pain, frustration and despair in dealing with loving someone with active addiction. I sacrificed much as many parents do in rearing their children. It is my quest of finding an answer to help him. The trials, the tribulations, the joy, the sadness has transformed my life to realizing it really is in divine order. It is my purpose in sharing this work of self-discovery with you so you too will see that every decision, every person, every thought in your life has lead you to this point on your sacred path. If one person is empowered or enlightened by my story then I have accomplished my mission. This is a story of faith, strength, and hope. I hope it will inspire others to find the **courage** that they need to meet the challenges that they face.

I raised both my children with the same values, morals

and standards. I always emphasized their individual gifts. Elizabeth was intellectually gifted and Nicholas was socially outgoing and athletic. It was very important to me that each child realized that they were special in their own unique way. I didn't want to raise them in an environment of competition. We all do the best we can- including me! I taught the children to be there for each other in good times and bad. Elizabeth grew up and attended an ivy league college and medical school on a full scholarship. Nicholas followed a vastly different path. Today, he works on his sobriety and maintaining a job that will someday offer him more opportunities.

When you read my story try not to judge me as a terrible mother or my son as an evil child. Fetal Alcohol Syndrome Disorder, drug addiction and mental illness are family problems and a national concern.There is an urgent need for FASD communities where adults like my son can live in a supervised, structured environment where they can maintain their independence and dignity.

"God grant me the serenity to accept
the things I can not change,

the courage to change the things I can,

and the wisdom to know the difference"

Reinhold Niebuhr (1892-1971)

CHAPTER ONE

Go with God

I was raised Catholic and, as most Irish children did in the 1960's, attended a parochial school from kindergarten to eighth grade. I argued vigorously when my mother wanted to send me to Catholic High School. Fortunately, my father was a staunch advocate of public education so that worked in my favor. My siblings were thankful that I, the oldest, paved the way for public education in our family. While in high school, I volunteered to tutor students with special needs and loved it. After high school graduation I entered nursing school and knew that I wanted to specialize in caring for children. It took several months of school before I concluded that teaching children was my true calling. To my parents' annoyance, I withdrew from the nursing program and embarked on my studies in education. Four years later, I was offered a position in a parochial school teaching 7/8th grade science. I did not have a science background but loved teaching the children, especially the ones who struggled. In my second year of teaching I meet 'Keith.' He was openly defiant to his teachers and had a reputation of being a very difficult student. Despite being a poor listener he was a smart eight year old boy. My heart melted for this little guy whose was being raised by his grandmother in a low-income neighborhood. Wanting to help Keith and other students like him led to my interest in special education and I decided to pursue a Master's Degree in that field. I attended a city college at night while teaching full time and tutoring part time. Salaries at parochial schools were so low we all needed to supplement our incomes. Finally, with a Masters degree in special education, I passionately entered the profession and obtained a position in the public schools as a special educator.

After establishing my career, I fell in love and married a Jewish man. Incorporating Jewish traditions into my life wasn't difficult. My parents, however, needed time to adjust to my acceptance of Jewish life. "After all," I told them, "Jesus was Jewish!" My strong relationship with God endured, I was simply expanding my religious practice.

A few years later we celebrated the arrival of our first child, Elizabeth. She brought so much joy to our lives that we tried to have another baby. It soon became clear that another pregnancy was going to be difficult. I tried infertility procedures and mourned each month as another chance to conceive passed in vain. Unfortunately, secondary infertility prevented us from making another baby so I began thinking about adoption. I accepted the fact that I was blessed with one biological child and was thankful. However, I believed I was meant to have another child. So, at the age of 35 I plunged into the adoption process with fervor. I told myself if it was meant to be it would happen and the process began flowing. Because my husband's family immigrated from Russia, we chose to adopt a Russian child. I found an agency that had children available for adoption. A personal loan from my father and a pension loan miraculously provided the much needed funding. We filed dossiers, were fingerprinted in triplicate, and in May of 1994 we boarded a plane to Moscow to adopt our son. I guess it's true that God helps those who help themselves!

CHAPTER TWO

Off to Russia

I n a journal entry dated May 22,1995 I wrote about my
upcoming trip to Russia to adopt Nicholas.

*"...The journey to Russia is about to begin. After so many
months-years it seems like my dream to adopt a child is coming
true. I pray for God's guidance."*

My husband, Joe, and I kissed our seven-year-old daughter,
Elizabeth goodbye and boarded a plane for Moscow to meet
and adopt our new son. We didn't realize where this adventure
was going to lead us. After so many months and years it
seemed like the dream to adopt a child would actually occur.
Seated in flight 102 to Helsinki, Finland we met three other
families who will travel with us to Moscow and Yaskarella.

We arrived in Moscow at 12 noon. What chaos it was!
We met our orphanage liaison, Ivanov, at the airport easily.
He had two other drivers so all of us piled into the three cars.
and headed to the hotel. There was no water at the hotel we
had reserved so we waited on the street for what seemed like

hours while Ivanov found us another hotel. We finally had a dismal room with two low cots and a functional bathroom. After resecuring our passports from the hotel, I called home to speak to Elizabeth and tell my mom where we were staying. I looked out the window on a city that was void of any color or charm and prayed that God direct us along our journey.

Early on May 24 we woke up, dressed and ventured to the hotel breakfast. After eating traditional Russian fare of black bread, cheese, salami and cabbage, we strolled outside to do some shopping. A little while later three drivers ushered us into cars and drove us to the train station. What a trip! The huge train station dated back to World War I with long military trains and military police standing guard with automatic weapons. Soon, we were sitting on our train looking out the window at a dirt poor countryside scattered with shacks.

The next day, we arrived at Yaskarolla and were escorted off the train by several drivers who took us to waiting cars. We proceeded to the orphanage with Nancy, the head of the orphanage. When we arrived Vadimovich, the Director, greeted us warmly. He was a lovely man! We were given a tour and met many children. Then we were escorted to the library and children's room where we met our son, Nicholas, for the first time. He was quite shy and would not look at us. We attempted to charm him, but he was guarded. He, along with the caregivers, sang a popular song to us. He sang so beautifully! At some point he let Joe pick him up and I could see the twinkle in Nicholas' eyes as he looked at me. At that moment I felt as though we were connected.

We were fed a breakfast of blintzes, chocolate wafers, apples and tea. Nicholas sat and ate with us. We told Nancy to go ahead and finalize the adoption while Vadimovich took us on a tour of the local river. With Nicholas sitting on his lap, Vadimovich drove us to the river and then to the children's camp.

Sonya, the orphanage English teacher, and I had a conversation comparing teaching in Russia and the States. She had two young children and kept saying she thought it was great that we were adopting. We went back to the orphanage where they had a big lunch prepared for us. A delicious meatball soup, bread, hamburger with a fried egg on top, potatoes, peas and a cherry compote were just a few of the options. I was very impressed with Nicholas' polite table manners. After we had eaten, Nicholas said "I'm ready to go. I'll drive us." We all laughed!

We proceeded to finalize the adoption and prepared to take our leave back to the train station. As Vadimovich and Nicholas gave good-bye hugs they both had tears in their eyes. It made me happy to see that he had been loved and cared for. We were soon back on the train for the eighteen hour ride back to Moscow, with our new Russian son.

It turns out that this was the hottest May in Russia and

there was no air conditioning. Nicholas played with the matchbox cars I gave him as he looked out the window at the countryside. I would bet he had never seen this area of Russia. At one point the train stopped and Nicholas ran down the hallway and almost jumped off the train. Luckily Joe grabbed him before he came to the door. The train continued on its way and our Nicholas finally fell asleep.

We arrived in Moscow and I immediately called our daughter so that she could talk to her new brother. Elizabeth, of course, said she couldn't understand a word he was saying.

CHAPTER THREE

Home with a Son - The Elementary Years

The first few months after we brought Nicholas home were filled with days of excitement and thrills for all of us. Going to a local toy store for a child is a fun-filled activity but, there were no toy stores of this magnitude that Nicholas saw in Russia. We piled into the car and took a family trip to the local toy store. As soon as we opened the doors of the store his eyes lit up like diamonds. "Oh my God!" he yelled and ran towards the toy displays. He raced up and down the aisles overcome with happiness. He pulled the biggest stuffed animal off the shelf and hugged it. Elizabeth my seven-year-old, was encouraging him to cuddle all the stuffed animals. He had the tigers, elephants, horses, dogs, and cats lined up in the middle of the aisle. We eventually gathered them up and placed them back on the shelves. He then ran to tricycles and bicycles, hopping on all of them, shrilling with excitement. At this time Nicholas spoke fluent Russian with a few English words in the mix. I always had my trusty Russian/English translation book handy. One of the workers came over to us seeing the total disarray. We explained that he had just come from Russia and never saw a toy store before. We told him we would straighten everything back to its original condition. Next Nicholas ran to the kitchens, castles, sandbox area where he proceeded to play with his new sister. His excitement brought tears to our eyes. We Americans take so much for granted and are so materialistic. We forget that there are poorer people in this world for whom having the basics is a miracle.

Taking Nicholas to the beach for the first time is etched into my memory forever. Imagine the first time you went to the beach and saw the ocean. For most of us it was so long ago we don't remember it. We took him to the beach for the first time in the summer of 1995 (five years old). As soon as his little feet touched the warm sand he started dancing with glee. He ran on the beach screaming with joy as we ran after him. When he reached the ocean he was squealing with delight. The look on his face was priceless. He raced into the water only to be knocked down by the waves. Nicholas was quite surprised. There were no oceans or beaches in the area of Russia where he lived. Nicholas continued dancing with the water for a period of time, each time going further and further into the ocean. I was a swimmer in the family, so I was right along his side with every wave. We joined him in his joy. It was a reminder for all of us how glorious it is to spend a day at the beach and how wonderful it is to swim in the ocean. Nicholas' first day at the shore touched our hearts once again.

I sent Nicholas to a private kindergarten in town. The open classroom allowed the children to roam from room to room. This seemed perfect for him and in addition there was a staff member who spoke fluent Russian. Perfect! In the first year we rationalized, along with the pediatrician, family, and friends, that he was settling into American life and customs. Nicholas was average intellectual functioning. He was well liked.

As more difficulties came to light, we had him evaluated. The evaluations concluded that he demonstrated reduced attentiveness, hyperactivity, receptive and expressive language deficits, visual-motor integration, memory deficits, oppositional defiance and poor impulse control. The violent and impulsive temper tantrums, the bouts of running away, and hoarding of food persisted even with doses of Ritalin. Neurologically he had meltdowns that only physically restraining him would calm him down. Socially he presented with many difficulties in holding boundaries (for example, walking into a stranger's house) and maintaining friendships.

I sent him to the local public school for first grade at age six. Once, when he was six and a half, he didn't come home on the school bus. My older child went to the same school. I returned home from work at 4pm and panicked, where was Nicholas? I eventually found him playing on the school playground. He continued to miss the school bus over the years, even with strategies in place. Often I found him at various classmates houses throughout the town. I was constantly calling or writing to the staff of the elementary school. He took frequent walks to the bathroom where he would either climb the wall or bother kids. We modified his bathroom privileges to only include using the nurse's bathroom. He would wander through the school building, talking to kids who were seated in class, punching kids, engaging inappropriately random impulsive acts. His lack of organizational skills were minor in comparison to his behaviors. Nick received speech therapy and counseling within the public school.

Nicholas[we started calling him Nick] was so adorable, yet I felt so overwhelmed raising him. I was in constant contact with his teachers, counselors and principals. I wrote so many letters that I could fill a 10-gallon Rubbermaid tub. I would cry at times and pray to God for help. I knew people that gave kids like him back to the adoptive country because they were just too difficult to handle, but I was committed to being his mom. The prescription of Ritalin temporarily slowed him down. We felt some relief. The outbursts remained a daily reminder of the challenging job of raising him. Our nerves were raw, our tempers flared. We isolated ourselves from each other in the pursuit of peace, however, this was an illusion.

There was no peace – not yet. Even with my background in special education, I could not fathom how this diagnosis would manifest in years to come. I speak from experience when I say I researched, explored, and desperately sought services in the areas of neurology, psychology, education, psychiatry, and pharmacology for my son. It became my life's mission and continues to be to this day!

The days blended into weeks and months. I was in constant contact with his elementary school. Behavioral contracts, private tutors, speech therapy and summer school was coordinated between soccer practice. We exposed him educationally and culturally to all of America our resources could offer. Academically he made great strides. Socially he presented many difficulties in maintaining relationships. We attempted social skills classes on the school level and private counseling. Play therapy was not the avenue to reach Nick's heart and soul. I was on the phone with my mother everyday relaying the daily drama. Trials of Ritalin, Dexedrine, Adderall, Tenet, and Prozac were initiated. I would chart behaviors and dosages. Success was inconsistent. Side effects would appear like vocal tics, picking of his nails, and loss of appetite. The psychiatrist at the time threw up his arms as he asked what prescription did we want to try now. I had a nagging sense that the behaviors we witnessed was more than "Severe ADHD". I researched Reactive Attachment Disorder books and articles and presented them to the psychiatrist. He dismissed me.

Luckily my principal and co-workers empathized with my difficulties. Countless times I would be in tears by the time I arrived to work. Nicholas set off the fire extinguisher or pulled a knife or ran down the block (even though we had additional locks on the door) all before 7:30 A.M. I was constantly getting calls at my job regarding his behavior. So, off we went on a two-and-a-half-hour ride to an adoption expert. We enlisted a new neurologist who instantaneously diagnosed Nicholas with RAD – Reactive Attachment Disorder – post-traumatic stress syndrome. He was quick with the prescription pad, but that's where it ended. It is a term used to describe the reciprocal behaviors between a mother and her baby as they learn about each other. For example, the baby cries and the mother picks up the infant and comforts them. The cycle is repeated thousands of times during the early years of life and when the mother responds to the baby's needs a sense of trust is developed. Attachment disorder can develop in infants who grow up in orphanages. Consequently, since they failed to learn reciprocal interactions with a mother figure they lack trust in adults to meet their needs. They experience much rage when they do not get what they want. Well that was Nicholas! He was abandoned at birth by his biological mother and left in the hospital. I do not know for how long. He was then placed in an infant orphanage till age three when he was transferred to a children's orphanage. One of the symptoms that we saw was lying. He would lie about something ridiculous. What I did not realize is that people with FASD lie because they do not remember the truth. He still does today and says that he tells people partial truth. He needed and still needs to be in control. According to Elizabeth Randolph, "Children Who Shock and Surprise," there are four basic types of attachment disorder… "anxious, avoidant, ambivalent and disorganized." Nick appeared to be" disorganized." He was openly angry and defiant. These children are superficially charming and can quickly change for no apparent reason into excessive anger - which explains all the holes in my walls and doors. He was destructive both as a child and later as an adult. Most disturbing is that these children engage in dangerous or risk taking behaviors that often involve delinquent acts.

In May of 1998, three years later, I took a three-month family leave without pay from my full-time teaching job. We were in crisis. There was trouble in school, on the bus, the playground, and, of course, at home. He would run away and I would find him in strangers' homes having cookies and milk. A symptom of RAD or so we thought. We put more locks on the doors. He would climb out of our windows and onto the roof. I feverishly searched the internet in pursuit of a miracle. We needed to take a loan to compensate for the lack of my income. I was overwhelmed and extremely tired. One had to physically restrain Nick to calm him down. I found a skilled therapist named Monica who specialized with "attachment issues" of adopted children. Finally, the puzzle pieces were forming a picture of a little boy whose abandonment at birth instilled in him a loss of trust and security, or so I thought. He preserved his selfhood and emotionally pushed away those of us who demanded intimacy. The gates of his heart were fragile. He fought off our love, especially mine, with the fortitude and strength of an army. We underwent weekly family therapy with Monica who was trained in "holding therapy" since traditional approaches of therapies were not working. This approach pushes the child to confront his beliefs about the need to be in control of others in order to survive. We learned different parenting techniques since the ones we used with Elizabeth did not work with Nick. I also did this at home by rocking him in a rocking chair, giving him a bottle and pretending that he was a baby and I the mommy was caring for him. He liked it and said to me often "I wish I came from your belly." He always had a way of touching my heart! Nicholas allowed himself to trust us more, to feel and give love, and of course, pain as well. This was a slow and painful process with many regressions. We persisted with the school district to accommodate his special needs and to awaken the staff to the complexity of his diagnosis. My husband tried to help. He would write up modifications, attend IEP[Individual Educational Plan] conferences, coach his soccer teams, but it was too much for him.

Nicholas's behavior would cycle. He would cry and complain of stomach aches before the sessions. He was still hoarding food and would occasionally steal things from others. We would have great days, weeks, and even months. "Great" is defined by fewer meltdowns. Neurologically he just could not calm himself down. I would talk to him calmly, sing to him, but I had moments when I would yell. That always proved to be the worse strategy. Nicholas would flip out and then I would have the job of calming him down yet again. It was best to be calm. He would scream, "I hate my family. I am going back to Russia."

Fetal Alcohol Syndrome Disorder (FASD) is the result of chronic alcohol use during pregnancy while Fetal Alcohol Effect (FAE) or Alcohol Related Neurological Disorder (ARND) may occur with only occasional or binge drinking during pregnancy. The degree of damage depends on the metabolism and liver functioning of the mother during pregnancy. A small amount of alcohol can kill brain cells[The Anatomy of Addiction 195]. Drinking during any of the trimesters causes permanent damage to the fetus. We were told that my son's biological parents were alcoholics, but we're clueless to what that really meant in raising a child with this diagnosis. I learned that the characteristics of FASD was low birth weight, small head circumference failure to thrive, developmental delays, organ dysfunction, facial abnormalities such as smaller eye opening, flatten cheekbones, indistinct philtrum, epilepsy, poor coordination of fine motor skills, poor socialization skills, behavioral problems including hyperactivity, inability to concentrate, social withdrawal, stubbornness, impulsiveness and anxiety, learning difficulties including poor memory, inability to understand concepts such as time and money. Individuals with FAS can have the same symptoms but to a lesser degree. The term Fetal Alcohol Spectrum Disorders (FASD) includes Fetal Alcohol Syndrome (FAS) and Alcohol Related Neurodevelopmental Disorder (ARND). Individuals with FASD often have symptoms or behavior issues that are a direct result of damage to the prefrontal cortex, which is the part of the brain that controls "executive functions."

I do not know why we did not recognize the complexity of his diagnosis at the time. Many of the symptoms Nick displayed seemed to indicate that Fetal Alcohol Syndrome Disorder[FASD] was the correct diagnosis. Both parents were deemed alcoholics by the Russian government. No medications can remedy this diagnosis. Symptoms can be medicated. I conferenced with yet a new neurologist. This doctor did research on my son's case which greatly impressed me. She was open to finding an answer to our medication problems. Dr. Donna did not possess a miracle drug, but she was willing to try risperdal or lithium. I really did not want to place my nine-year-old son on these strong drugs. Nicholas's genetic history was not provided in great detail and he was already displaying vocal tics. As the thought of giving my little boy lithium was just too frightening, I chose to give him the risperdal. I was juggling the medications to get a more desired effect. The schools didn't fully cooperate with me when I requested that they monitor Nicholas's behaviors during the new drug trials. They weren't always consistent with reporting behaviors. How could I try lithium with him if they couldn't monitor ritalin and clonidine? Always in the back of my mind was the daunting thought that if you do not reach kids like Nicholas by their teenage years, problems with drugs, alcohol, the law, and sex would prevail and the battle is lost. Believing myself to be an optimistic person, I hated to think that could be true. Every January his behavior started to deteriorate. He was threatened at school with suspension for fighting and had bus suspensions. The only playmate I could find for him was the boy next door. He didn't even want to play soccer. He spent countless hours watching television and shutting the world out. By May, his behavior seemed to improve. That particular academic year was more stressful for me than him. The professionals didn't appear to have the strategies to control his behaviors or address his academic deficiencies. When I conferenced for his IEP (Individual Educational Plan) I was in tears. What else can I do for him? I requested a personal aid at school for him. Some personnel were supportive, reassuring me he doesn't require a self-contained special education class. I was worn out. Over the years some of my professional friends tried to convince me to place him in that type of classroom. I was and will continue to be my child's advocate. However, the cost was great. In hindsight, I should have placed Nick in a self contained special education class. I tried desperately to be reassigned out of my special education position to a mainstream teaching position. I tried to apply for other non-teaching positions, but was told I needed more seniority. Finally, I turned in papers to take a leave of absence (without pay) so that I could find a position in the same state as I lived. Teaching children with learning disabilities/ADHD and living with a child with severe needs was making me crazy and burning me out.

I enrolled in the local college that summer taking supervisory courses so that, in the future, I could obtain a position as a supervisor of education. I secured a teaching position closer to home in hopes that this would be the change I needed to make my life a little simpler. I needed to be closer to my children, especially Nicholas. So, in my selfish pursuit to strive for a new position as a supervisor, my college courses intensified, his anxiety increased. He spent quality time with his father and sister but I believe he felt I was abandoning him. Trips with him to the beach and pool became exercises in patience and my personal strength. I was back to three or more physical holdings a week in public places. I have to tell you at 43 years of age I was not keen on getting down on the floor and restraining him. I had gotten over the public humiliation and stares, but this was wearing me down physically and emotionally. Nick would physically retreat for hours watching television, unless I was in his face demanding interaction. Any change in schedule are difficult for kids like Nicholas. He started to get into physical fights at camp and having trip privileges retracted.

He was approved by the local County for Special Children within the first year we adopted him and was appointed a case manager in 1996. The case manager proved to be a good resource, especially when Nick was suspended/expelled from the community schools and recreational programs every school year. It was recommended to me to communicate with the state's Special Advocacy Program. They were not able to get him back into the summer recreation program, but they provided phone numbers for attorneys that dealt with special needs students. I sought advice from the top attorneys in the state.

Eventually my courses ended and he seemed to return to a more connected, obedient child. We spent a week at a restful resort in Florida, a vacation we all desperately needed. The last third of the vacation had become a "rad" adventure. The most difficult behaviors are seen in children who were prenatally exposed to alcohol and who suffer from Reactive Attachment Disorder, according to Debra Evensen. That is the truth! Nicholas had decided that he didn't require parents and was doing his own thing. If we say ``no," he did it anyway. It took physically removing him from the situation as he was yelling and kicking to calm him. Oh, I mourned the passing of summer and the onset of school for Nicholas and myself. What hurdles will we have to jump this school year? The transitions are always a challenge. One day at a time has become my mantra.

By February of 2001 the family situation was pretty bad again. My soon-to-be-ex had a close encounter with death. Nick had a "zero tolerance incident" in school while we were waiting for his father to be discharged from the hospital. Nick was ten years old. He told some girl he was going to bring in a steel bat and beat her. He would get angry when kids told on him and then his out-of-control rage took over. The school appeared to handle the situation gently with him. The other parents were outraged over the incident, of course. Nicholas kept saying he didn't remember when he was questioned about the incident. Needless to say he needed psychiatric clearance before he could re-enter school. I made over fifteen calls during this time to various professionals. I kept a journal and kept count. It was therapeutic to write. One psychiatrist recommended a mood stabilizer like Depakote. He told me that I needed to monitor his behavior. I thought that was what I was doing. I was only seeing a private neurologist, psychiatrist, counselor, and then the school's team of counselors and psychologists. How much more monitoring could I do?

Suggestions for finding help:

Public Schools [Social Services Department]

Play therapy and Holding therapy[google for private therapist]

Local Hospital's Division of Child Neurology and Neurodevelopmental Division

Social Security [local office]

County Division of Children's Service

Mental Health Association ·

NAMI

Association of Mental Health and Addiction Agencies, Inc., (NJAMHAA) Division of Mental Health

CHAPTER FOUR

Junior High and High School

I separated from my husband of seventeen years, which added to both children's emotional distress. Nicholas received private counseling for many years from various professions in specialties such as reactive attachment disorder, abandonment/adoption, holding therapy, drug/alcohol. Sadly, all that counseling did not prevent the cycles of drug and alcohol addiction that would transpire. From the onset of age thirteen, Nicholas found himself in altercations with the local police. The oppositional behaviors escalated from lying and stealing to leaving the house in the middle of the night. He attended juvenile counseling for trespassing on public property and stealing and had several months of juvenile probation. I also requested a male mentor from the local police department in hopes of redirecting his behaviors. Nicholas was easily manipulated by peers and drawn to trouble. He destroyed property when his rages of anger took over and punched holes in my walls. Both of my children attended their individual counselors to help ease with the divorce and their relationship with each other. Nicholas was extremely problematic and frequently involved in physical altercations.

In eighth grade, 2005, Nicholas attended share time in a vocational school in the afternoons. He had previously received a report card filled with D's. He attended the local junior high in the mornings. He started to have behavioral problems in the public school and the Vocational Education Placement. Nicholas's behaviors consisted of lying, stealing, cursing, and oppositional defiance. I was on speed dial with his therapist and the school as well as still teaching full-time. I signed so many consents so that everyone's therapist could talk to each other and then talk to the school personnel. It was truly by the grace of God that I was able to survive each day. Nicholas was with a female counselor for two years and so I switched him to a male that I hoped would be more beneficial.

The psychiatrist changed his medication cocktail again. This time it was Trileptal (a mood stabilizer) and Strattera. He was caught smoking cigarettes in school and didn't show up for detentions. He told them he couldn't find the detention room. I got numerous calls from the Vocational Education school. He had poor performance, little effort and his interactions were poor. They said I might try counseling. Were they kidding? He never stopped seeing a counselor and psychiatrist. He ended up failing the special education vocational classes, even with an IEP and modifications. We found a male counselor, Dr. Silver. I called the crisis intervention mobile unit hotline begging for help. I spoke to the most seasoned doctor there that had some experience with the complexity of my case. I called my case manager at the County's Special Child Services begging for assistance. Division of Developmentally Disabled wouldn't service Nicholas yet. What, he wasn't disabled enough? The system was frustrating, and even though I was a Special Education teacher with friends in the field, I couldn't get the needed help for Nick.

There is no doubt in my mind why adopted parents relinquish their adopted children in cases such as mine. When the public read in the New York Times and heard stories on TV such as Hansen's sending back their seven-year-old Russian son in 2010 and consequently Russia halted adoptions in January 2012, they truly do not understand the challenges and obstacles raising an FASD child. I, with a Master's Degree in Special Education and a special education teacher with numerous professional friends in the field of education and psychology had an overwhelmingly difficult journey in raising Nicholas and receiving services. What chance do other parents have? According to NO-FAS "FASD is more prevalent than Down Syndrome, Cerebral Palsy, SIDS, Cystic Fibrosis, and Spina Bifida combined. Alcohol use during pregnancy is the leading preventable cause of birth defects, developmental disabilities, and learning disabilities. FAS/FASD has lifelong implications. As noted by the Institute of Medicine's 1996 Report to Congress on FAS, 20 out of 10,657 babies born a year have Fetal Alcohol Syndrome. 1000 of these babies are born with Alcohol Related Neurodevelopmental Disorder. The comprehensive lifetime cost of just one baby with FAS could be as much as $5 million. The cost to American taxpayers for FASD is estimated to be over $5 million A DAY!

According to Muhammad in The Anatomy of Addiction, people with FASD have problems planning and organizing their daily lives as well as comprehending the consequences of their impulsive behaviors.[197] I believe what is needed in the United States is an expansion of public education of FASD children and services that are actually readily available to assist families in raising all these children. FASD is more than an adoption issue. It's a global concern with the abuse of alcohol and drugs in our society. Most children with FASD have inappropriate sexual behaviors, show poor judgement, have difficulty controlling their impulses, are emotionally immature, and need frequent reminders of rules. As a result, many will require the protection of close supervision for the rest of their lives according to Teresa Kellerman.

Damn it, I was determined to find a way to reach Nicholas. I was on the phone with the state advocacy program and the insurance company attempting to get these new therapies covered. Did I mention that I also went for therapy and prayed feverishly those years? Nick continued to misbehave at school and at home, breaking all the rules and curfews. He'd sneak out of the house in the middle of the night and then make up some story when he got caught. I lost so much sleep through those teenage years. "Thank God for coffee!" was my mantra. He, of course, refused to do homework, which I may add was the least of my problems, but he would do whatever he wanted. I punished and grounded him and he still was out of control. He was picked up by the police for possession of a knife. I beseeched the local police to have him spend the night at a juvenile correctional facility. The school heard about it the following day and gave him in-school suspension and searched his locker for weapons. I was questioning why the school got involved in police matters which occurred after school, but I found out that is what they do. Soon after he stole a cell phone, an incident that was filmed on camera and a school administrator saw it. Rest assured, at this point everyone knew of the tales of Nicholas and he was frequently guilty without being charged, and maybe rightly so. The principal gave the tapes over to the local police. Now it was an out-of-school jurisdiction. I soon found out that there was an incident at the high school football game where Nick apparently stole $50.00 from his friend. His friend chased him into the high school where a cop just happened to be and spoke to Nicholas about the incident. Nicholas's friend didn't want to press charges because they were friends. I spoke to Nicholas and with tears in his eyes he said he was sorry. What a manipulator! I later found someone's credit card in Nicholas' pants. I destroyed it. I didn't know what else to do.

I interviewed attorneys to represent his cases of theft. The best case scenario was that he would be on probation. Months go by with the common adjournments of court dates. My ex husband was not supportive to me at this time, but rather blamed me for Nicholas' problems. On recommendations from yet another psychiatrist, Nick went on a trial of a black label drug (Strattera) Within a few weeks Nicholas started talking about killing himself. I called the S.W.A.T. team of professionals. His world was spiraling down and he was drowning. Eventually, he was admitted to an Intensive Behavioral Facility. Here they took Nicholas off of all medications, observed his behaviors, and reassessed his pharmacological needs. He spent a week there and was released the day before Thanksgiving.

Who suffered here? Me. I had to go to work to earn money so that I could support my children and deal with this constant craziness. In hindsight, I should have kicked him out then or put him into foster care, but I couldn't. I signed up for this parenting gig and I was committed. Nicholas's lack of insight and impulsive behaviors was not my fault, nor was it his. The professionals told me Nick's lack of cognitive understanding and lack of cause and effect were the results of FASD.

Nick was seen at a local IOP (Intensive Outpatient Program) where they evaluated him. Smoking pot and drinking were in the mix now. I was told that with FASD as children age different symptoms appear, there is no cure and that stimulant medications will not work. What was now needed was psychiatric drugs. Reluctantly I had him placed in a more restrictive environment. The public educational system did not address his intense behavioral and educational needs. They happily allowed me to choose any school that I felt might help meet Nick's needs. Nick required a placement where he was academically challenged and had available, on a daily basis, counseling in a highly structured and behaviorally consistent environment. In ninth grade he attended an out-of-district school where he did receive what he needed. I might have pushed for residential school. Those were the relatively quiet years in school. Thank you, Jesus.

However, Nick's police incidents increased in town. Another new neurologist, drug trials of Abilify, and counseling with Dr. Silver. I begged my ex husband to take Nick and that I would pay him child support. Yeah, that went over big. More temper outbursts, destroying property, and smoking pot in various locations in town, and always around cops. Nick's standardized testing scores came back from the state indicating that he read at an eighth grade level but math skills were at 6.6 (five years below) with language mechanics at a 3.9 level. Mind you, he was almost 17 years old. The private special education school re-administered the state test to him again. He needed to pass the state test, otherwise he would get an IEP diploma. I advocated to get him vocational education again, this time in a different county. So many calls were made to so many different agencies, my head began to spin. The local county didn't want to take him back after their experience with him when Nick was in eighth grade. Now, three years later, they still remembered him. This time maybe a different school would bring him success. He started in a new county vocational tech school.

I started to investigate "guardianship procedures." All the professionals that I was taking Nick to agreed that I should pursue it, but I had reservations. Nick got a part-time job in a local food store. At first he was placed on the registers, but after a period of time Nick said it was too much pressure, so he got demoted to carts. More lies, more deceit, hanging at the mall instead of the job, and getting into fights. The job lasted for close to a year until he was fired.

By his junior year in high school he was truant from school so often that there was a fear that he would be retained. He purposefully missed the bus that came to the house after I left for work at 7:00 A.M. I was trying to get him to stay in school. Under IDEA (Individual Disabilities Education) Act he had until the age of 21. I contacted the director of special education in my local school district. Was there a better placement for Nick? They were clueless as well. One

30

of the realizations I had at the time was the $50,000 a year tuition and the $10,000 transportation fee the district spent on Nick's yearly guaranteed him to graduate. He could not budget money, fill out a job application legibly, make phone calls or use other executive skills that were needed to be self-sufficient, but those were minor issues in comparison to his behaviors. Unfortunately, problems with FASD intensify as the child moves into adulthood. These include inability to live independently, trouble with the law, drug and alcohol abuse, and developmental health problems - and my boy was a textbook case. The services available for FASD in my state were sparse. It was easier to apply to my private health insurance and have him deemed a permanently disabled adult than to get any help from the state agencies.

Suggestions for finding help: Most state provide these services

Division of Vocational Rehabilitation Services [DVRS] -[located in most states]

Department of Labor

Mental Health Mobile Crisis Teams

NAMI-National Alliance on Mental Health

Criminal Justice Advocacy Program-The ARC

Department of Human Services-Division of Developmental Disabilities

CHAPTER FIVE

Beyond High School

O n Nicholas' 20th birthday I wrote,

…" There isn't a day that goes by that I don't pray to God or thank God or ask him to take over. I feel like I'm always praying to God during my day. Thy will be done seems to be my mantra as well as the Serenity Prayer. I feel I can't get through the day without God. And yet I feel that my life is divinely guided! Perhaps some may say that I use God as a crutch but for me I could not withstand all that I have had to endure without God's help."

It took from 1995 to 2010 to finally get my son eligible for services with the state Health and Human Services Division of Developmentally Disabled. Did they think he was not developmentally disabled? The only service they offered Nick was to be placed on the list for residential placement that might occur in the distant future. The year after high school Nick was 19 years old and getting high most of the time. I asked him to leave the house multiple times so I could motivate him to go to rehab. Each time I locked him out, it got a little easier to ask him to leave (locking the doors, changing the locks). He stole cash and jewelry from me. I didn't press charges because an addict always finds their own trouble. I was regularly attending "the program." My son was in intensive outpatient and inpatient rehabilitation on six separate occasions in a dual diagnosis facility over the course of two years. During that time, alcohol and pot seemed to be his drugs of choice. On one occasion the local rescue squad came to my house after he passed out from alcohol poisoning. I called a friend at midnight and together we watched as the EMTs took him to the local hospital unescorted. I didn't pick him up the following morning, but rest assured, one of his friends did.

With all my attempts to intervene over the years, I could not circumvent the consequences or the ramifications of his organic brain damage, FASD. Unfortunately, even his Russian born psychiatrist did not get the criminal system to understand his disability. According to No Fas there is a need for "development of the necessary screening, analysis, and treatment procedures for those with FASD who enter the foster care, juvenile justice, or adult criminal justice system. Intervention training for professionals who work in high risk settings such as clinics, addiction centers, psychiatric wards, orphanages, and jails." His psychiatrist and I collaborated on a letter that we sent in an attempt to educate the court system.

I remember having a feeling or premonition of doom on one particular evening and asked Nick not to go out. Of course he did not listen to me. The local police knocked on my door the following night at 3:00 A.M. wanting to bring him in for questioning. He was arrested for aggravated assault in the fall of 2010, a year after graduating high school. I did not post bail, but rather I hired him another attorney. After all, he was looking at a felony. The bail bondsmen would call me relentlessly all day describing what Nick's cell looked like or what he was wearing. They were vultures preying on a parent's love. Nick threatened to kill himself and got moved to the psychiatric jail cells. Again, the correctional facility called me. "What do you want from me?" I asked, "Don't give him shoelaces." People told me to hire a lawyer and give Nick a second chance. They couldn't count too well. Nick's attorney told me he was not running a group home when I begged for the guidance and assistance from the Developmentally Disabled Offenders Program on Nick's behalf. I attempted to enlighten this attorney, but they know what they know. The jails are filled with FASD/FAS inmates that went astray. He ended up serving less than two months in the county facility. I shiver at the thought of what might have occurred if I did not intervene.

The Division of Vocational Rehabilitation Services in conjunction with the Department of Labor provided services in the summer of 2011 where Nick received 100 hours of basic skills/career assessment/career preparation training. The small stipend he received enabled him to have some spending money. I drove him daily to the local community college. At the completion of the program he was placed in a neighboring adult vocational school in the plumbing trade. This was the most beneficial and practical service provided. Luckily, I was able to pay one of his classmates to drive him to the program as I was still trying to work full time in another state. It took him twice the amount of time to complete the plumbing technician program. This qualified him to earn appropriately $10.00 an hour. He eventually would need to further his training and education at a vocational school in order to move forward in becoming a licensed master plumber. Nick did not seem able to complete the application to initiate this process to get into the union. I offered assistance multiple times and he refused to allow me to guide him or motivate him to follow through with the process. In 2012, with help from his father and me, he was able to buy his first car.

In September of 2013 he was arrested and found guilty of a DWI charge. He said someone slipped him Ecstasy in his drink. When I asked him why he would try to drive impaired, he said he thought he was okay to drive. It was a miracle that no one else was hurt. Once again I hired an attorney to represent him in court along with the assistance of Developmentally Disabled Offenders Program in my county. I did not go to court with him that day because once again, I hired an attorney and he had an advocate. They told me that they would oversee his compliance with the consequences of the drunk driving charge during his license suspension. I drove him to work at 6:45 A.M. each morning so I could make sure he got there and he managed to get a co-worker to drive him home most days. I encouraged Nick to apply/ obtain a second job to help him pay the many fines. Instead what I noticed was that he would be out every night and pissing away every dollar he made at his job lending money to"friends." People affected with FASD have great difficulty with understanding the value of money.

It became apparent to me that Nick was drugging and drinking again. When I questioned him as to why there were empty beer cans and liquor bottles thrown in the bushes behind my house, he responded by telling me they weren't his. Nick said, "Maybe they belong to the girl next door." They happened to be the kind of girls that didn't party. His continuous lying stemmed from both his addiction and his disability. He told me he doesn't have a problem since he goes to work every day. So, now he is was a functioning alcoholic. The day I discovered that he was selling pot out of my house I asked him to pack a bag again and leave. He was not only committing an illegal crime that broke his probation, but he was jeopardizing my safety and livelihood. His poor impulse control had taken over again. At first he checked himself into a motel. His sister and I found him a room to rent that was local and clean. Instead, he rented a room from a druggie friend's sister in town. "It was cheaper," he proclaimed. I saw him, supplied an occasional meal and attempted to guide him (like to attend AA meetings). I loved my son dearly and it saddened my heart to see the path that he had chosen. I could sleep at night though, because I knew in my heart and soul that I did everything possible to help him. I was not certain what the future will hold for Nick. I only hoped that he'd become self-sufficient enough to live outside of my home and avoid any further illegal activity.

He was living out of in my house for three months when he lost his job in February. Two weeks later he told me his landlord was going to jail because she broke probation. I believed his story and I let him come home temporarily. I really didn't know what the best plan of action was for Nicholas' independence. I know that turning over problems to God is the answer for me. It gives me peace of mind. I don't lose sleep mulling over the details and situations to nauseous. Live and let live or is it let go and let God. Either and both. It serves the same purpose. My son, for the past eight years, has been dealing with chemical/alcohol dependence and criminal issues. He has been in rehab on six separate occasions in a dual diagnosis facility. It has been unsuccessful because he doesn't really want the help and maybe he also requires a Mentally Incompetent Chemically Addicted (MICA) program that may actually turn his life around. Unfortunately, the criminal system and the medical field do not always converse.

Years ago when I became involved in the Nar Anon program, I received much peace from the slogans they preached. I still do. Somehow I found the strength to survive the years without being on serious drugs or being committed during Nick's many drug and alcohol addictions/relapses and the consequences of those behaviors over the years. There were arrests, juvenile interventions (that worked not at all), probation, in-patient rehab, outpatient rehab, DUI, license suspensions, and let's not forget fines and legal fees. Oh yeah, about $10,000 in legal fees is what I spent in order to "do the best thing" for him. I always prayed to God before I make a major decision.

Just in case the life of Nick wasn't enough to test my faith, I had an ex-husband that did not understand Nick's intense special needs. He filed a motion in 2013 to emancipate Nick and terminate child support. Logically you would think that a 23-year-old should be emancipated, but I believe not in this case. The court decided that Nick wasn't ready to be emancipated as of yet and that child support could be reduced since Nick was working for minimum wage. In the process of this procedure Nick was arrested for DWI, lost his driver's license, sold pot out of my house, was kicked out by me and living with a woman that, as it turned out, was on probation as well. The court system is funny about having two people living together on probation. Not to worry. By the time I found out, Nick had lost his factory job that took him over a year to obtain he had the services of the Division Vocational Rehabilitation to assist him. When you have no skills companies don't exactly jump up to hire you. The night Nick told me that his landlady was going to jail because she broke probation I had a moment of weakness. I told him he could come home temporarily. Honestly, I just couldn't take all the drama. He told me he lost his unemployment benefits after six weeks. I attempted to provide posted rules that I had discussed with him prior to his return to my home. You go mom! I was still dealing with our son. Am I to send him off to a shelter and tell him to dine at a soup kitchen? I found this situation totally overwhelming!

In July of 2014, Dr. Alison asked me if I wanted to take medication to relieve my anxiety. I said I am kind of opposed to medications. I do yoga and meditate. Wasn't that good enough? She suggested therapy. I am a veteran to counseling of all sorts. I explained to her that I went to therapy for close to twenty years for my son, my relationship with my ex-husband and myself. That worked, right? Actually it did. I told her I get overwhelmed. It's no wonder that I feel depressed, overwhelmed and suffer from a lack of focus at times. It doesn't last long and I think it's situational. Modern medicine suggestions are if you aren't going to take a pill, then go to therapy. The doctor had no idea of what my life was like raising a child with FASD. My prescription on this is that I need to deepen my meditation practice, pray to my angels/ higher self and have more faith. After all, I believe God helps those who help themselves. That is not exactly what is taught in medical school. I left the office with the thought that I would go back to therapy. Hell, it's been a year or two since I last attended sessions. It's an opportunity to have someone just listen to me as I ramble on and on about my son. They won't tell me what I should try to do or that I should kick him out of my house. They won't segue into their own personal sagas. Oh, why not give it a go? In the meantime, I wrote down my concerns and placed it in my God box asking God to take this problem from my worrisome soul. I wonder why I get a bit depressed at times with my life. I just can't imagine. Are you sensing the sarcasm? I have juggled more balls in the air simultaneously for so long that I can't remember anything else. It had gotten easier in a sense with my sons growing older and one out of two living independently. It's not a pity party, but rather a clear picture of my reality. My father use to say, "God doesn't give you anything you can't handle." I don't know. I think God is a bit ambitious with me. Perhaps he overestimated my staying power.

For six months, Nick worked with a job coach from the Division of Vocational Rehabilitation Services and ARC (Association for Retarded Citizens). He finally landed a job and was so excited to be working again. The smile on his face was huge. He woke up every day at 6:00 A.M. to leave by 6:15 in order to drive a few towns away to get to work time. Mornings and punctuality are not his strengths, but he was getting it done. I made sure that he had a lunch to take and that he took his medications in the morning. On the fifth day he arrived at the job site only to be told that they were evaluating the temp workers and he could go home. He would be called if he was going to be one of the three employees they were hiring. He came back to the house deflated. Luckily, three days later he was assigned a different temp job. I texted his job coach the news. I encouraged him to be persistent and tell them he will work any hours. However, DVR may not continue assisting him with coaching because he took a temporary job. I told the job coach he can quit it then if that is an issue. Did you ever? Can you believe the nonsense of these agencies?

My heart broke for him. It was so difficult being Nick! It was difficult being me! I heard it in his voice when he said he hates his life and bad things only happen to him. His view of life was more simple than most people. He was unable to plan for the future even if that future only meant tomorrow. Nick couldn't set short-term goals, so long-term goals were a foreign thought. What could a parent do in a situation like this? How could I walk the line of encouraging independence and providing guidance and direction at the same time to a 24-year-old man/child. I prayed for guidance and direction.

I prayed for patience in dealing with his disappointments. He had $800.00 of bills/fees to pay each month because of his DWI charge. The financial burden fell on my shoulders if he couldn't make those payments. His dad only agreed to pay $400.00 a month while he is unemployed. Again, I thought "hand it over God."

As life would have it, Unemployment sent Nick a letter stating that because he was discharged for misconduct on his job he was ineligible for unemployment benefits. So I sent a letter to Unemployment asking for an appeal of their decision. Here is an excerpt of that letter.

Sarah (his job coach from ARC) was responsible for getting him this job and she was not allowed by this company to come on site to help/guide Nick. In fact, it took over a year to obtain that job. It was against his civil rights under I.D.E.A.[Individuals with Disabilities Education Act] that Sarah was not allowed to help Nick keep his job. Sarah can be contacted to confirm any of this information.

> Now that he was fired, your agency is stating that he is ineligible for benefits because of misconduct. He was fired because of his cognitive impairments/developmental disabilities to understand time. He was late to work. It seems to me that his rights were violated here.

Nick has no money, no job, and now has no unemployment benefits. Now I will be forced to apply for Social Security Supplemental benefits. The goal is to have him independent of the system not totally dependent on the system. This is not right or fair.

I am requesting that he is WAIVED OF THIS DEBT on the bases of .A.C.12:17-14.2 (permanently disabled). I am enclosing a statement from my medical insurance carrier as well as DDD eligibility letter that states he is disabled. If you would like more proof of his disability, I can provide truckloads. In addition, I am requesting that his unemployment benefits be reinstated due to the violation of his civil rights. It was one thing to pause the benefits for six weeks, but another to terminate and demand that he pays the benefits back that were disbursed."

Where did I find the strength to continue battling this downhill spiral? "Hey God? HELP! Send an angel or two to hold me up when I crumble in despair," I prayed, "And include an angel or two (or S.W.A.T. team) for Nick to show him the way to law abiding independence!" I received a letter from

Unemployment stating that Nick had a telephone hearing on the matter of "Discharge for Misconduct: Discharge for Severe Misconduct." I explained to Nick what it was all about. I proceeded to write an email to the concerned parties to try to get the documentation that was kept by his ARC job coach during his employment. Here is a copy of that email.

Dear Debbie,

Nicholas, my son (for whom I have Power of Attorney), was assigned Linda. He was hired in March 2013. After, Linda left ARC, Nick was not assigned another coach that visited him on his job site. No one at ARC, I believe, had any information on Nick's progress. He was at the job from March 2013 to February 2014. He was dismissed (let go) in February 2014, at which time he applied for unemployment benefits. While he was employed she attempted to visit him at his job site. She was not allowed on site nor would they speak to her. She attempted several times. I am sure this must be documented in the notes that were kept on Nick.

Nick has a diagnosis of FASD/Developmental Disabilities with time management, impulsive and generalization of rules and consequences major deficiencies. Nick received Unemployment benefits from------to and then they were frozen for six weeks. On July 11 he received a letter (Notice of Determination) stating that he was discharged from his job due to "violation of company rules and is misconduct."

I filed an appeal on his behalf when Unemployment wanted to recoup the benefits paid out in the amount of ---------- under the WAIVER OF DEBT: A.C. 12:17-14.2. This indicates permanent disability. I sent them documentation from DDD (Division of Developmental Disables) and Power of Attorney form. I will fax them more documentation on his disability. I will attach the letter I sent to Unemployment. He now has a telephone conference on August 8, 2014 with an Appeals Examiner.

I would like a copy of the notes that indicate Linda attempted to visit the company. I believe that Nick's civil rights were violated under IDEA. I have a call into at DVR (Division of Vocational Rehabilitation) as well. Nick was released from his job due to his disabilities.

The state agencies (ARD and DVR) were not allowed to assist him in order to retain the position.

Now, since he applied for Unemployment benefits he is being discriminated against in receiving those benefits because of his disability. He recently worked for two and a half weeks at a temp job (that I found for him) in order to earn some money. This system is totally ridiculous.

Thank you for your assistance in this matter.

A week later I went to see the psychiatrist who had seen Nick for almost eight years. I originally chose him because of his Russian medical education and that he was knowledgeable on FASD. He prescribed various drugs for Nicholas over the years to assist the mood disorders, explosive behaviors, hyperactivity, and impulsiveness. He said, "I don't know what to tell you. I don't have any clients like him in my practice." "Thank you very much, that was helpful," I thought, "What am I to do with that?" No one seemed to know if his behavior was due to addiction, FASD or both. I called the supervisor of the case manager that they assigned me at DDD. A lovely, young, clueless woman. I loved the help I got from state agencies.

In August I went to a retreat weekend. It was peaceful and

relaxing. I met many women of like situations. By Saturday night I had a feeling that I should leave and go home. I generally trust my feelings, so I packed up, said my goodbyes and left at 9:00 P.M. As I approached my house, I saw that all the lights were out and yet there were many cars parked in front. I just knew Nick was having a party. I tiptoed to the back of my house where I saw a group of guys drinking and getting high. I walked into my house and saw that my dining room was transformed into a beer pong room. The look of surprise on Nick's face was priceless. He tried to tell me that he wasn't drinking beer and that his friend was smoking synthetic pot. Actually, he was too high to talk, so his friend did most of the talking. I calmly told him to clean up. His friends mysteriously disappeared within ten minutes. Nick asked me, "Are you going to kick me out?" I calmly said, "I will think about it and get back to you."

I called his dad and told him that Nick has to move out again. We decided we would help him look for a room to rent and make this a positive experience. We looked for a month while Nick did very little to assist this process. He was too busy getting high, we just didn't know it. His dad was finally getting involved in parenting now as he had not been involved for many years in assisting me in raising Nick. Now that he was, I was thankful because I was just too tired to deal with this alone anymore.

CHAPTER SIX
The Big "H"

The weeks of late September and early October were a never ending rollercoaster ride with hair-raising whips and stomach-churning turns. I was emotionally worn out and physically tired. I wanted to run away and never return. Life started spiraling downward on Monday, September 22nd. Nick's father came over to look for rooms to rent and fix the car. Before leaving, he gave Nick some cash. Earlier that same day Nick was at my house asking to shower and work around the house so I gave him $20 for weeding the flower bed. After that, we didn't hear from him for a couple of days. When he finally did call, he said he was working a double shift. That Thursday morning, September 25th, he knocked on my door at 7:15 A.M. stating that he worked overnight and needed a shower. I let him in and gave him a cup of coffee and let him use the shower. I wasn't in my "lock down" state of mind since I was only half awake. He took a quick nap, and then asked me if he could do anything to earn money. I told him

I have no cash and need to work more myself. Next, he told me he needed two checks to pay Catholic Charities. I told him I would write them and send them out. "Oh, I can drop them off," he says. My checkbook was in his field of vision when he asked me for some Scotch tape. I still wasn't putting the pieces together. Abruptly, he states he needs to leave for a job interview and runs out the door yelling "I'll see you later, Mom." Little did I know that "later" would be the following week when his father briskly escorted him to my backyard.

A few hours later I sat down with the checkbook to write out the checks for Catholic Charities. I quickly realized that the two top checks were missing and my immediate thought was he stole them. Then I thought "Maybe I had a 'senior' moment?" I searched through my checks and thought I counted them or numbered them incorrectly, but I wasn't seeing a mistake. I felt terrible thinking he would do such a thing even as I texted his father to tell him my suspicions. The following day, Friday, I searched my monthly statements and saw no renumbering. I even drove to the bank and questioned them. They reported that I needed to come in and file a report. I waited until that Saturday morning, because I had a nagging feeling that if he wrote a check for a huge amount, it would totally screw up my account and my mortgage. I went into the bank, and low and behold, he wrote a check and cashed it for $200 the day before. He didn't sign my name, but addressed it to himself. I placed a hold on the other cheek and filled out a report for the check that was cashed. I was furious. I texted him and told him that I knew he stole the checks and if he cashed the other one he would be arrested on sight (bullshit, but it sounded good). I also told him to stay away from my house. I was done.

Outraged, I called his father, who actually was sensitive to my anger and said, "I don't blame you for being angry, but do you really think pressing charges and having him arrested will help him get a second chance?" We didn't hear from Nick until Tuesday. He sent a quick text to his dad telling him not to come visit because he had to work. Nick didn't know Joe had already arrived. Suspicious, Joe drove to Nick's temp agency and questioned the boss. The boss said he hadn't seen his son in months because Nick hadn't worked there in months. Joe searched around town for Nick and eventually found him at his girlfriend's house. He brought our son back to my house where we attempted to have a conversation but Nick was too high to speak.

On Wednesday, Nick got arrested for his second DUI and was taken to the local emergency room. I called Joe and he came into town to meet me at the ER. We both refused to sign the hospital release because we wanted Nick to be admitted into a drug program. We talked to him for an hour and, of course, he denied using drugs and alcohol. His girlfriend took him to her place and his car was impounded. The next day, I took Nick to the hospital to get a copy of the medical report and go to Catholic Charities to pay for the program that Nick was in but barely attended. I looked at the medical report and saw that he tested positive for opiates They were discharging him and returning the case to IDRC. On Friday, I picked Nick up and drove him to Social Services while I waited outside. I took him for breakfast and he went into the bathroom for 15 minutes. I noticed he wasn't eating much and then I saw a red mark inside his elbow and I thought, "he is shooting up!" We discussed detox and I had him call several detox facilities. He said he would go and made an appointment with his Probation Officer because he was out of compliance for not checking in. The PO needed to see him or she would send a warrant for absconding. All weekend long we didn't hear from him. We had an appointment scheduled on Monday at 1:00 P.M. for him to be admitted to a detox facility. He never showed up and didn't answer our texts or calls. It was all set up. I had a bag packed in the trunk of my car. His probation officer told me that they would issue a warrant for his arrest since he's missed probation for close to a month. I left him a message saying, "I love you. Don't destroy your life. It can all be fixed in time. Call me so we can take you to rehab." Finally on Monday afternoon, a very drugged Nick answered his phone stating that someone was dropping him off to the probation officer.

Nick "talked the talk, but he didn't walk the walk." Everything with him was a sea of lies and deception. I didn't fear death for him, rather, I feared him living in a vegetative state, hooked up to ventilators and feeding tubes. In fact, I texted him and told him to write "Do Not Resuscitate" on a piece of paper and place it in his wallet. I didn't know if that was a program step, but it was a "Mom has had enough of this!" step. I prayed for his soul, for his recovery and for the three of us to have the strength to deal with whatever came down the road.

I had two calls into my new sponsor. I felt so restless and exhausted but couldn't sleep. A feeling of foreboding hung over me. Was it just my anxiety or was it a premonition of the future? I saw Nick lying in a coffin at his funeral. It saddened me to have such a horrific vision. No mother wants to have that image of their child, but then he wouldn't be in such pain – on a soul level – in the grips of addiction. It was such a disastrous scenario. Finally on Tuesday, Joe got a call from Nick that he was ready to go to detox. Joe picked him up, drunk and stoned, and drove him to detox where I met them. The clinic finally admitted him. Because Nick denied that he was high, the insurance company would not pay since it was not "medically necessary," We were charged several thousand dollars for the stay at detox.

There was a sense of peace and calm while he was in detox. Calls were limited and visits were not allowed, which was fine with me. I needed some time to step away from everything. Nick was discharged from detox a week later but where would he go? He couldn't come home with me or go to his father's house. We thought perhaps a shelter so Joe drove him to residential rehab facility. He spoke to a manager but it was late and the offices were closed. The man said he would squeeze Nick if we brought him the next morning. Joe placed him in a hotel and took his cell phone. We prayed that he would still be there the next day. It was a miracle that Nick didn't leave that hotel room. The following morning Joe picked him and took him back to the shelter where he was finally admitted after hours of waiting.

I knew the realities of using heroin were not good. In my mind I saw what the outcome could be. I hoped that it won't be his outcome, but somehow I felt that I needed to prepare myself on some level. I prayed that he would truly embrace rehab, but I cannot trust his words. They have all been lies. There was no trust in our relationship. I prayed for strength that I, his sister and his dad could weather whatever storms were to come. I couldn't be sure if Nick was truly honest with his recovery. He was facing the law and his noncompliance with IDRC, the new charges of DUI, his violation of probation, loss of license for years and, of course, all the fees. The best thing would be drug court ordered by the judge. At least then there was a chance that he would stay in rehab longer. I wondered about his Dad stepping up after all these years, was it a sign of worse things to come?

His plan was to transition to an Intense Outpatient Facility/

Sober Living where he would be in an intensive outpatient program at the local hospital. It seemed to be an ideal location for mass transit, since he had no car. Nick wanted me to donate his car so the taxes he owed from unemployment could be balanced by a tax deduction. The fees he faced for all his legal troubles were expensive and would stretch on for years. Additionally, he had to deal with the local courts and IDRC for the violations of DUI/DWI. Nevertheless, he was excited and nervous about this next transitional phase, as we all were. He had to fully embrace the fact that he was an addict and would be for life. The wisdom of the program, and changing the people, places and things in his life will assist his recovery.

Nick had been in the halfway house for several days when I received a call from him telling me that he wanted to leave his Intensive Outpatient therapy early every day so that he could find a job. I found this disturbing since he had only been going to IOP for three days. He continued to tell me, "Mom, I heard all of this when I went to IOP before." My response, which I couldn't stop myself from saying, was "Yes, and that worked out well for you. You graduated to heroin. Are you kidding me? Your recovery is the most important thing right now and not getting a job." The following Thursday was his court date. It had been rescheduled and the halfway house was allowing him to attend. His father graciously agreed to pick him up and take him back and forth to court. I met them there in order to give Nick some important papers. They read Nick his charges and he asked for a public defender. Being oblivious and detached from the consequences of his actions, he was shocked to find that he was facing criminal charges.

Three days before Thanksgiving Nick called to let me know that he was allowed to leave the halfway house from 8:00 A.M. to 8:00 P.M. on Thanksgiving Day. He wasn't up to seeing any family and needed to be checked in by 8 PM sharp so I made reservations at a nice restaurant for just the two of us. It would be a less traditional Thanksgiving for me without my family and daughter, but I decided that spending time with Nick was my priority. On Thanksgiving day I picked him up before noon. I brought his dress shoes and jacket to wear at the fancy restaurant I had chosen for our Thanksgiving dinner. We arrived at the restaurant and were seated upstairs in a charming room with poinsettias and a fireplace. We perused the menu and he decided to order a hearty steak dinner. I was so thankful to have him sober and straight and in recovery. As the meal progressed, Nick said he had something to tell me. I usually cringed when he said something like that because it was never good. He said the day before he went into detox he passed out after shooting up heroin. He told me he saw a white, foggy light. There were two white shadows there motioning for him to follow. He started to follow them, but then the distance grew farther and farther. He said he felt safe. He then woke up and was angry because his friend was throwing water on his face and slapping him to get him to wake up. Nick said he looked in the mirror and saw that he was bleeding from his nose and ears. He said he knew he overdosed and died that day.

I cried and explained to him that he had a near death experience. I remember feeling the previous Monday that he was in a bad place. I saw him in a coffin. That is when I turn to God. God's will, not mine. This was where the strength of the program would comfort me and peace would fill my heart and soul. What else could I do?

Suggestions on where to find help:

Local Nar-anon and Al-anon meetings

Social Services [SNAP, Medicaid and general assistance]

Private psychiatrist and addiction counselors

Catholic Charities

Local and state Mental Health Services

CHAPTER SEVEN

Escape to Florida

By August of 2015 Nick had been six months in an Oxford House, a national recovery house. I usually saw him once a week for laundry or dinner or both. The Oxford House was going to kick him out because he wasn't working full time. They had spoken to him several times [which he did not share with us till much later] that he needed to work more than his part time job at the car wash. They said his noncompliance with house rules jeopardizes everyone's sobriety. Nick claimed he had applied for jobs but was having a hard time finding work. He was coasting along on food stamps and his parents paying the rent. I felt that was a huge mistake and his father and I disagreed as to when to cut off his financial support. We were more concerned with his recovery than we were with his work ethic. Nick was content to get by on little money so he spent his days hanging out, which is destructive for an addict.

On a particular sunny, hot August morning he informed us of his plan. He had apparently relapsed and found a detox facility in West Palm Beach that was sending him a plane ticket and he'd be leaving in a few days. Very interesting. I was quite surprised! Not so much about the fact he relapsed but, that he had managed to execute a plan for his escape. It amazed me that he was able to orchestrate this move, but not find a full time job. He sold his clothes, furniture, and of course, my laptop. I dropped him off at the airport feeling relieved that his problems were moving with him to another state.

In the course of the first 5 weeks I rarely heard from him. I would text or call him and he rarely responded back. It was difficult for me to understand what was going on with him.Sometimes I felt used or hurt and other times I was able to detach with love and felt relieved! Detaching from the addict is a challenging venture. Human nature is to care for your kids and help them. In the case of an addict it is called "enabling". It is such a fine line and a delicate dance. I found comfort attending my meetings and listening to others share their challenges of detachment.

Nick bounced around from facility to facility until December of that year. I told my children that we would all be together for Christmas. My older daughter was living in California. I paid for a plane ticket and took out insurance. I had concerns that he wouldn't board the plane. I was delighted and relieved when I meet him at Starbucks in the San Francisco airport on that December 22. It was the first time that I had seen him since August. It was even longer for the kids. We stayed at Elizabeth's apartment with her boyfriend and celebrated Christmas like we always did each year. We visited the sites of San Francisco area, and shared meals and laughs. We were a family!

Nicholas looked healthy. We all noticed the "track marks" on his arm that we thought looked too fresh. He claimed it took a long time for them to disappear. Honestly, it's close to impossible to trust an addict. I left California a day earlier than Nick. I wanted the kids to spend some more time together and it was cheaper to fly Nick the following day. I was brought to tears as I waited for my flight in San Francisco airport. I have spent my adult years mothering these kids and it saddens me to see us live so far away from each other. Was I suffering from that empty nester syndrome perhaps? Between Elizabeth 3000 miles away and Nick 1500 miles-tears filled my eyes. The Christmas trip was a success and that I was thankful for.

Nick moved to yet another rehab[#4]. When I made calls to the facilities to get a mailing address so I could forward the reimbursement checks from the medical insurance I usually got a different version of the "Nick story." During one particular call I was informed that Nick left to go to a facility that allowed drinking and smoking weed. Rehab reinvented! The crazy scams that were occurring at these rehabs in Florida were outrageous. One facility billed my insurance $84,000 for Nick being there for 3 months. Seriously, I could have had total body overall/reconstructive surgery at least once. There is no way these rehabs warrant that kind of money. When this facility couldn't get their $84,000 from the insurance they had the nerve to bill me $42,000. Really? I sent them a pointed response. To this date I think my insurance did eventually pay them $32,000. I spent hours reviewing the "explanation of benefits" and making copies of reimbursement checks. Handling the insurance claims alone was a full time job. In April, Nick moved to rehab #5. I was dizzy! We might have spoken weekly, if that. As usual, he proclaimed he had a sponsor and attended NA meetings. I had no real clue as to what he was doing.

I missed him but was extremely relieved not to have to deal with his daily life. I decided to fly down for Mother's Day to visit him. I had anxiety! I arranged a car rental and a friend graciously offered the use of her condo for the weekend. I drove to his "sober living house" praying the whole time! He told me he was the new house manager. Ok. He didn't have 1 year of sobriety but apparently that was not an issue in Florida.When I pulled up to the house I was appalled at how rundown and dirty it was. Nonetheless, I was relieved to see him.We spent three wonderful days together exploring the local beaches of Delray and West Palm and their eateries. On Mother's Day Nick gave me a beautiful heartfelt card and a gift card to Starbucks [my favorite coffee house] that brought tears to my eyes. When I boarded the plane to return home. I was happy that I decided to visit him. I had missed my son even knowing that he was high during my entire stay.

Nick asked me if he could fly home for his birthday in June. He had not been back home since the prior August. I lamented and decided he could come home for one week. Of course my anxiety increased as the date drew near. I put the house in "lockdown mode' -hide checkbooks, credit cards, and money in my locked bedroom. I told him my 'rules'[no drugs, alcohol staying out late]. It helped me to establish boundaries. My older daughter and her boyfriend were flying back home for part of the week. I thought it would be great for all of us to spend time together.

I picked Nick up at the airport on his birthday. We spent a nice day together. He had lunch with me and dinner with his dad. He informed me he was seeing friends later that night. I thought he said he wouldn't be seeing friends but he complied with the midnight curfew. All was going well so far. As the week went on he would call me sometime before midnight to tell me he was sleeping over at the house of one friend or another. Although I didn't notice any overt signs of drug use I remained suspicious. It was a difficult situation because I did not trust him. My children spent some time together in the city with their dad and with me. I enjoyed having my children around. As Nick boarded the plane to return to Florida I felt a sigh of relief. It was very challenging having him visit and stay in my house. I realized that I suffered from "post traumatic stress syndrome." I forgave what transpired but, I had not forgotten!

By September, Nick was complaining that he was going to be evicted in a month because this "halfway house" was relocating to Del Ray. Nick, because he no longer had my "golden pass" medical insurance was told he would have to leave. I finally cut him off when he refused to let these facilities talk to me. Perhaps it was dramatic but, I needed leverage. I asked Nick what he was going to do because I wanted him to manage this crisis. He said he would look for a place to live. In the meantime he was working as an assistant mechanic for some garage in West Palm Beach. The owner paid him for the first week. Nick was so excited that he was learning how to do oil changes and brake jobs. The owner had him work more hours but all he got was partial payment or the promise of getting paid. Nick refused to leave this scumbag. His dad and I tried explaining to him that the man was taking advantage of him and that he shouldn't work for someone unless he is getting paid. Apparently, the garage owner had filled Nick's gullible head with talk that some famous rapper was going to buy into the business. Nick, realizing that he had been conned, was asking for my help. He wanted to come back home. His father and I encouraged him to apply for food stamps and medicaid. I called the Housing Authorities of Florida seeking some assistance and they suggested going to the local Social Services. Meanwhile, help would take weeks before starting.

I went into high gear. I started to research agencies that could possible help Nick. I called Easter Seals and started an application. I called the Division of Mental Health and was basically told that if he is a client of DDD (Division of Developmentally Disabled) he has to go through them because his primary diagnosis is no "mental illness." That was debatable! I called Catholic Charities. They would have a "path worker "contact Nick. [Side note-their worker did call Nick several times but Nick choice not to return the call]. They did not want to speak to me. Okay! I was told that Nick needs Social Services first in order to get any assistance.

I called the local county SERVE, and was told the waiting list is a long one. I called "At Risk Housing" agencies and got the verbal run around. Volunteers of America put his name on their waiting list for housing. I called the County Program Director. She informed me that priority housing goes to those individuals who are discharged from psychiatric hospitals. I then called CPC Behavioral Healthcare. Again, I was told there were no openings for shared apartments. Most clients stay in the apartments for a long time.Who can blame them? It takes so long to get accepted why would they ever leave? I called the County Division of Housing, I was told they are just gives housing vouchers. I was told that the vouchers go to the homeless first. Nicholas was homeless and could go to a shelter but I really didn't want to see my disabled son in a homeless shelter.

I contacted DDD [Division of Developmentally Disabled] and was assigned a caseworker who turned out to be helpful. Nick needed to be reassessed by the Developmental Disability planning Institute. He completed the assessment electronically with my assistance in early November. I am still waiting for their psychologist to contact him so they can do another assessment and its mid December. Not so helpful! I find it an extremely frustrating situation to get Nick who has a developmental disability, mental illness and addiction issues any HELP! I researched Oxford Houses as a possible residence. His dad and I agreed to pay the first months rent helping him to get established. According to NO FAS "Further contributing to the lack of recognition are federal, state and private insurance disability classifications that do not consider FASD as an eligible condition for services. A lack of understanding from the general public adds to housing and employment difficulties, making many adults with FASD dependent on their caregivers." Trust me I am his wing man!

CHAPTER EIGHT

Return from Florida

E nabler or parent? I flew him back home with the understanding that he had 10 days to find a job and a place to live. On the night of October 22, with all his belongings in plastic bags, he arrived at the airport. Early Monday morning we were at the local Social Services offices. He reopened his SNAP [food stamps] and Medicaid account. We then proceeded to the Social Security Office. I had applied for Social Security for Nick many times over the years and was always denied for one reason or another. Luckily, there was a cancellation for the following day for an assessment appointment. My work schedule was light and the changes needed were simple enough to make this appointment. He needed to go back to Social Services for a General Assistance interview on Wednesday. GA is a ridiculous program where the client is required to show up at their office for 40 hours a week for a month in order to receive $120.

I fed Nick lunch and we proceeded to check up on the

status of his job that he had arranged while he was still living in Florida. He was cooperative. When he told me that his eyeglasses were broken. I made a call to my union to check if he was covered for a new pair. Score one for mom, he was covered and they were sending the certificate in the mail. Replacing his eyeglasses twice a year has been an ongoing activity for years!

Next was the Oxford House interviews to set up. I filled out the forms and made calls and had Nick do the same. I think his head was spinning with all the activity.The following morning we were back to Social Security where we spent two hours being interviewed. The case was being reopened. We searched rooms to rent and made interview appointments at the various Oxford Houses. Every interview seemed to have problems for Nick. The jobs were either not easily accessible by public transportation or they rejected him. I watched as his 'cooperating mood' dissolved into the old 'oppositional attitude' I have known for years. At the end of the day he found a room to rent in a town neighboring his job. It was through "a friend of a friend" and not my concept of ideal but, it afforded him his independence and my freedom. It was a stressful two weeks having Nick live with me. I was constantly locking my bedroom door and looking for my keys. Perhaps, I did not have to take these measures but, as I mentioned earlier I have post traumatic stress syndrome and did not forget the events of the recent past.

Nick claimed to be tired of living in a rehab environment. He had been living in rehab/halfway houses for 3 years and my response was "well, you didn't quite get it if you are still wrestling with addiction." I knew I should shut my mouth, but sometimes the sarcasm just spewed out. He informed me the reason he wasn't so keen on living in a sober house was because he smoked weed. "Mom, it's not a drug!" he proclaimed. By some miracle, two weeks to the day after he came home, his dad and I moved him into his new rented room. The house he found was so permeated with cigarette smoke that I had a severe headache after a few hours. I did my best to scrub yellow film from the doors and windows. Then, we set up his temporary air mattress and assembled a dresser. Nick was happy.

I took him to a local bank to set up an easy pay debit card. Since there was a local bank alert on him because of what he owed he was unable to open a checking or savings account. Nick agreed that I should help him save money but that lasted all of two weeks. Some days he would ride a bike to work, other days he would take a cab. He bounced from one temporary factory job to another and ignored our advice to try to stay at a job long enough to earn some credibility. However, he did what he wanted to do.

Eventually, Nick found a full time job with a moving company. It was fortunate that one of his co-workers was able to drive him to and from work. In exchange for the ride, Nick bought him cigarettes and gave him gas money. Nick was living as independently as possible at the time. At least his job seemed more stable than all the past three factory jobs he had since he returned from Florida. Nick was happy to be working and felt good about himself which was so important for his esteem. One of the reasons I did not aggressively pursue social security supplemental support for him was I wanted Nick to be as independent as possible. Additionally, idle time is too dangerous for an addict, it gave him more time to drink, smoke or use drugs.

Nick decided in January 2017 that he was going to move in with his then current girlfriend and her two kids. His father and I tried reasoning with him that this was not a great idea. We felt it was odd that he was now dating the twin sister of his former girlfriend. The family had many members who battled addictions including their mother. The girl was looking for financial support for raising her children as well.

I helped him move from the rented room to the new two bedroom apartment. They were paying one thousand dollars a month for a two bedroom apartment which was a step up from the smoke filled room he rented in some older man's house. I gave them old dishes, pots, pans, linens and whatever else I could. I collected other people's throw aways/giveaways just for this purpose. Nick did laundry at my home on Sundays and they would all stay for dinner. I didn't mind initially and it gave me an opportunity to chat with them.

At first, he really seemed to love being a 'pretend dad.' He played with her children and was loving to them. The kids called him"daddy." They acted like a family. I thought Patti was clean, sober, paying the bills and into being a full time working mother. She set up a cozy home for the four of them and liked to decorate. I actually began thinking that maybe this situation was working out and enabling Nick to grow to be a responsible adult. It did for awhile. I knew he was not exactly clean and sober but, it appeared under control and he was working full time consistently.

After he lived with Patti for a month or two I started hearing stories of them partying at the local pub on the weekends when the kids went to their father's house. It became obvious that they were regulars and would often host after parties at their place. It interfered with their ability to pay the rent and utilities. Soon, they were served with an eviction notice. I told Nick I would not be able to help him pay the back rent, eventually Patti got the money from the children's grandparents. As time passed, Nick spent more time at my house on the weekends or out with friends. The kids were out of control, crying all night and no one got any sleep. The older girl demonstrated some emotional problems like biting other kids at daycare. I tried to speak to Patti several times about establishing firm rules and being consistent with time outs but I guess it was too challenging. Kids having kids does present many difficulties. Patti had no one to mentor her[besides me] in her family. Nick really could not say too much to the children and that frustrated him. It was no longer a happy family of four and Nick did not have the tools to cope with a bad situation. He had not learned healthier coping mechanisms even though he had been to rehab several times. Instead, he partied more and came home less. Patti started calling him"stupid" and yelled and belittled him in front of her kids. I felt so sad for Nick, I never wanted life to be so hard for him. He started life with too much to bear being born to an alcoholic woman and abandoned at birth.

One Friday, he called me asking if he could sleep over my house because Patti was having her new boyfriend sleep over. There went that commitment. Of course, I allowed him to stay the weekend so I could nurture him with home cooked food and encouraged him to move away from the girlfriend. It was finally decided that he was going to move out in December. We had plans to fly to California to spend Christmas with my daughter and her fiance. Nick, myself and his coworker, moved his belongings out of the apartment while Patti was at work. Because of his generous heart, he left his furniture and linens behind for her and the children. I also gave her a gift card for food because her food stamps were paused. Little did I know, she sold the gift card for cash.

I told him he had a few weeks at my house to resolve the living situation. Because his executive skills were so poor I knew it would take longer this time and I would have to intervene. Hopeful, Nick moved into my guest room and we organized his meager belongings.We traveled to California and had a wonderful holiday with his sister. However, his earlier return home was a great source of anxiety for me. In the back of my mind, I knew there's a huge possibility he would party while I am away. I also knew I had no control over what he did when I wasn't there. The Nar Anon program teaches the 3C's. I didn't Cause it, I can't Control it and I can't Cure it! Such a simple concept yet, so difficult to master! I would relapse into old behavior at times by trying to cure it by sending him to a rehab or control it by not allowing drinking at my house. With the help of my many years of being in the program my relapses are shorter in duration and when I feel weak I get myself to a meeting, do my readings or call a member.

After my arrival home from California I assisted Nick in his search for a room to rent. I knew he felt safe in my comfortable home but it was not the best option for him or me. I always felt somewhat anxious when he lived with me. Too many years of living with his active addiction scarred me perhaps. Nick needed to be as independent as he could be. Our home town was a trigger as his party friends were here. Nick had not attended NA or AA meeting so he did not have sober friends to hang with. Trust me when I say I strongly encouraged him to get a sponsor and attend meetings. I knew I couldn't control his recovery! It was his path.

Two weeks evolved to two months. I called, made appointments, and drove him around to look at available rentals but we found nothing suitable. I think I was trying much harder to find him a place than he was. Finally, I told him I was changing the locks February 1st and he wasn't getting a key. Nick needed a bit of a kick in the ass to motivate him. I believe he was too busy with partying with a new girlfriend. He always had a girlfriend. He's cute, attentive and women seem to be drawn to his charms. He even got them to pay his way! By the grace of God we finally found a room to rent in a neighboring town. I had to lend him some money for the two months of security this landlord demanded but, it was a small price to pay for my peace of mind. Besides, I had managed to save almost $1400.00 of his money. I drove him over to meet the landlord and amazingly, the house was cleaner and newer than the last apartment that he shared with last girlfriend and her two kids. I wasted no time in moving him right in. At this point he had no bed and I wasn't buying another one right away so I gave him my queen size air mattress for the time being. We made the place livable. I have learned that when boundaries are set, we have to live within them. I knew Nick was still getting high but I chose not to live with his active addiction.

Life seemed to be going smoothly during January and February. Nick reluctantly gave me some of his earnings to save for him which was necessary as he had no money management skills. Unbeknownst to me for several weeks, Nick lost his job in March. I found out when I told Nick I would be needing his help during a few weeks in April after I underwent hip replacement surgery. It one of those rare, fortuitous moments when he was able to care for me for two weeks and collect unemployment. Nick was a very patient and loving person and a wonderful nurse to me during the first week of my hip replacement recovery. He stayed and helped me until I was able to do more on my own or with occasional visits from friends.

Nick went back to Tony's house and his rented room. I saw him less and less. I can't recall exactly when I received the explanation of benefits from my medical provider in May stating that Nick had received ER services via an ambulance. It started making sense to me that he was telling me he wanted to go back to rehab. When I questioned him why he responded that he couldn't stop smoking pot and had not paid May's rent. I found out he had a seizure due to smoking pot laced with K2. He was lucky that was all that happened. I calmly explained to Nick that, like so many others, he could have died or worse ended up in a wheelchair drooling on himself! He complained that he hated living in the rental house and having to share one bathroom with five strangers. I encouraged his desire to re-enter a rehab and found him a selection of in network facilities in neighboring states. Nick decided to go to a rehab in Pennsylvania and moved out of Tony's house at the end of May. Thank goodness I was physically able to drive again so I could assist him in the move. He spent a night at my house and the next day, June 3rd, I whisked him away to the facility. It was a dual diagnosis residential facility and it appeared that he would be provided with the services he needed. He seemed to be motivated with his approaching 28th birthday and stated he wanted to get his life on track. Seemed like a win-win solution to me!

CHAPTER NINE

Florida and the Future

Nick stayed in Pennsylvania for a month and then relocated to an affiliated step down program in Florida. In Florida, he lived in an apartment with another sober male, attending NA meetings, and worked part time. He appeared happy and proud that he was"'getting it together." Unfortunately, when something, big or small, went wrong in his life he cycled downward and relied on drugs and alcohol to make himself feel better. He had two relapses while he was in the Partial Hospitalization Program and was placed on medications [Strattera and Lamictal] to monitor his moods. The last incident saddened me to tears. He found out that in order to retain his drivers license he had to pay $6,000 in fines in addition to the rehab time he was doing. That realization threw him into a downward spiral. He asked his boss for money because he wanted to spend a weekend with some girl he met. The boss put two and two together and told the Rehab facility. When Nick arrived back to the rehab facility Sunday night they drug tested him and found cocaine in his system. He lost his job and was sent back to residential components of the rehab. He claimed he looked for another job but, I had my doubts. The insurance company only approved Residential Rehab for 5 days at a time. In Nick's case, it was never enough time.

He eventually signed himself out of the Florida rehab and moved back to his home state to live with friends. I knew he was not clean and sober when he decided to live with friends that he had previously partied with. He started drinking and smoking pot again but, was at least working. Then months later, his roommates kicked him out because of a misunderstanding with a girlfriend.

Soon after, he met a woman at his work and he began to date her. She was previously married and had three young children, one of whom was special needs. She allowed him to move in with her and her children but laid down strict rules to Nick that there would be no drinking or drugging or he was out of her house. About a month later, Nick was admitted to the hospital because of an abscess on his foot. Maria and her children were visiting with Nick when I first met her. I liked her immediately. She was a hard working single parent that was determined to make a better life for herself and her children. I felt unbelievably relieved that he was with this woman whom, like me, was tough.

As time went on she encouraged him to apply for a

different job that had more opportunities for growth and advancement. He miraculously managed to obtain a drivers license from motor vehicles after he installed an interlock device on her car and set up a payment plan with the DMV for the DWI fees he incurred. He applied for the different position, was called in for an interview and started with the new company within a week. Nick has always been wonderful with children and he adores Maria's kids and treats them kindly. He is working diligently to learn a new trade and trying to make a better life for the five of them. Maria is in charge of the monies and paying the bills since Nick is not diligent with that task. I truly believe Maria is an angel and admire her strength and courage.

I hesitate to write too much about his current situation because I fear the unknown. I am cautiously optimistic about his future but also realistic because he has never embraced the Narcotics Anonymous program nor is he medicated for his impulsive behavior. In my opinion he does not use the tools of the program or a sponsor. I have lived through too many "Cycles of Nicholas" so I am naturally skeptical. Nick continues to use poor judgement in making some decisions even when Maria and I strongly encourage him to choose differently. Honestly, it frightens me but, it is out of my control.

AFTERWORD

God's will, not mine. This is where the strength of the Program comforts me and fills my heart and soul with peace. "Keep coming back….It works if you work it." May you be filled with hope! May you feel stronger and know that you are not alone in the struggle with loving an addict. I hope you become an advocate for abstinence from drugs and alcohol during pregnancy.

I certainly think that it's more challenging for Nick to stay clean because of his disability [Fetal Alcohol Syndrome Disorder]. I was able to insure him under my medical insurance as"a permanently disabled adult." I have applied for Social Security a ridiculous number of times. At first, I was told that he wasn't eligible because I received child support at the time. Afterwards, they determined he's not"disabled." They must be joking! There is only so much time I am able to spend diligently filing papers and duplicating medical forms. I even had various conversations with a Social Security attorney because I couldn't do it alone anymore. The goal was always for Nick to maintain gainful employment so I stopped the process. He needs to be busy and productive so boredom and a poor self image does not call him to back to the euphoria of drugs. It is a good thing that I am semi-retired because Nick requires much assistance and time.

For people like Nick with FASD [a victim of someone else's addiction/mental health issues] and addiction issues it is a lifelong challenge! Group therapy is usually not helpful, because of the risk of imitating unhealthy behaviors of others in the group. Cognitive therapy and insight therapy are usually not helpful either, unless the therapist has a really good understanding of FASD issues. One-on-one therapy may work, but often the problems are not psychological as much as they are neurological. A mentor that meets with the individual on a daily basis may be more effective than traditional counseling, according to Teresa Kellerman's <u>Substance Abuse Programs for Individuals with FASD</u>.

Throughout all of these incidents, I prayed for guidance and attended Nar Anon meetings. I speak at local conventions and a local rehabilitation family programs in order to be of service. The Nar- Anon community was there for me when I first entered the room years ago and now it is my time to give back. Nick's path is a challenging one that cycles every couple of months. It is his path! The path of someone afflicted with addiction is riddled with challenges and saddled with FASD as the primary diagnosis it is close to impossible to recover but, all is possible with God!

As Stephen Hawkings stated "as long as there is life- there is hope." May you find your serenity!

"Inspired"

APPENDIX i

In attempting to provide structure for Nick these are the rules I discussed with him before he returned to my home in the early years.

Nick's rules for staying at home:

1. CURFEW – be home Sunday – Thursday by 10:00 P.M. and Friday – Saturday by 1:00 A.M.
2. Clean room and bathroom weekly.
3. Give mom $100.00 a week for room/board as long as you get unemployment/job.
4. Give mom $75.00 to save weekly as long as you get unemployment/job.
5. No friends in the house unless I approve.
6. Do errands/chores at home as needed.
7. No Drugs/Alcohol.

APPENDIX ii

Here is an excerpt of my response to the motion that was filed by my ex-husband in August of 2013.

NJ STATUTE – TITLE 2A:34-23

1. Needs of the child

The (1) "Final Individual Plan" and (2) "Adaptive Behavior Summary" for Nick provided by Mr Z, Case Manager with the Department of Human Services, Division of Developmental Disabilities Community Services (DDD) is included in this discovery. In addition, I am supplying the (3) case narrative and (4) Individual Plan for Employment (IPE) issued from the Division of Vocational Rehabilitation Services generated from Sarah to support Nick's "disabled" status. Developmental Disabled/Fetal Alcohol Syndrome Disorder is a permanent disability. It's unlikely that Nick will make great strides to be a "functional adult".

As per "the Final Individual Plan" for Nick, Mr. Z documents in the Life Plan Summary section that "Nick needs help with financial matters and looking for work." In the Residential section, "Nick was placed on the priority waiting list on March 21, 2012 and that he should continue to live with me in the meantime. In Work/Program/School section, "Nick should continue with Support Employment Services/DVRA." In the Clinical Information Section all medications and doctors are listed as well as diagnosis. In the Guardianship Review Section, "Nicholas gave Mother Power of Attorney with Mother providing support in all areas of finance, medical decisions." In the Supervision section, "recommended that Mother continue supervision of Nick." In the section Additional Support Services, "Nick should continue with current levels of support/CM, Mother, DVRS." In the Additional Important Information section, "due to the recent changes in DDD eligibility, there is a need to apply for Medicaid in order to receive DDD funded services." Nick may never make more than what his salary is currently. This program would be in Nick's best interest. Finally in the last section, Action Required Summary, "Mother is listed for all actions required (current living arrangements, finances, medical, power of attorney, supervision, transportation, medication, and to continue with current levels of support, etc." Indeed, there should be no doubt for anyone to see that Nick is disabled. The evidence indicates that he "is under the sphere of parental influence," and "not functioning financially as an emancipated adult."

Nick still demonstrates neurological meltdowns and explosive behavior. With all the statements and bills that have been generated since his DUI, he is unable to read and follow the directions in order to comply with the directives. He only has a debit card and is unable to maintain any savings. He becomes overwhelmed and shuts down. He was constantly getting overdrafts. He has no money management skills and cannot fill out a check or a money order independent. Nick was unable to call the car insurance company to inform him about his suspended license without my assistance (I made the call). He requires reminders to pay bills, lock doors, make dental appointments, etc. without supervision. Adults with Nick's diagnosis have severe deficiency with money, time and executive skills. His math and reading skills are far lower than his age normalcy and socially he acts many years younger.

I have been repeatedly told by professionals that Nick will always require my supervision. Nick has been diagnosed with Fetal Alcohol Symptom Disorder – an irreversible condition, developmental delays, learning disabilities (especially in math and reasoning), hyperactivity, vision and hearing problems, inability to plan, memory issues, attention span, compulsive disorder, bipolar, poor problem solving and poor judgment. He has received psychiatric and psychological therapies since 1994.

2. Standard of living and economic standards

The majority of the 23 year olds in the United States are not "free of their parental sphere financially" in today's economy. How many disabled 23 year olds are "free of the parental influence financially"? Nick is not one of them. Nick may never make more than what his salary is currently.

5. Need and capacity of the child/adult for education, including higher education.

Nick needs to further develop his skills with a trade. I am not sure that he is capable of achieving this.

6. Age/health of the child/parent

7. Income, assets and earning ability of the child

Nick is making $12,000 a year (if he works full time without missing time, which he has missed several weeks since his employment started in March 2013). He has no assets, savings, or medical insurance of his own. He has a non-running 12-year-old car. He has no skills (the plumbing technician would warrant perhaps $10.00 an hour if he could secure a position). He does not have the cognitive ability, motivation and perseverance to further his training/education so consequently what he is currently making is his potential at this point. The poverty guidelines for January 2011 for a single person was $11,490 year

. Certainly, Nick's income places him in that economic class.

Nick has no responsibility towards his own maintenance. The Division of Vocational Rehabilitation obtained Nick his position at THE COMPANY six months ago and a job coach to supervise his employment. This was his first job since December 2011 and his first full-time job.

8. Responsibility of the parents for the court-ordered support of others

9. Reasonable debts and liabilities of each child and parents

10. Any other factors the court may deem relevant

I understand that the State law defines "the age of majority for a disability in economic terms, in that the disabled adult child cannot adequately care for himself/herself by earning a living by reason of mental or physical infirmity." The State Division of Vocational Rehabilitation Services classified Nick as "priority 1 – individuals considered to be 'Most Significantly Disabled' due to the disability that limits you in ways that result in significant impediments to employment" (Exhibit 6). Nick has granted me "general power of attorney" because he understands his cognitive limitations (Exhibit 7). He is still under "the Sphere of Parental Influence" financially, medically and psychologically as the document describes.

APPENDIX iii

According to Kidsave.com 62 percent of orphans in Russia are adopted by Americans. Russia had one of the most popular international adoption programs. In 2007, according to adoptionknowhow.com 700,000 to 800,000 children were abandoned in Russia. Worldwide 1.9 per 1000 births are born with mental retardation and behavioral problems due to alcohol abuse. In the United States, the economic impact of FASD (Fetal Alcohol Syndrome Disease) was appropriately $8000,000.00 per child or $321 million per year. Alcoholism, according to the National Institute on Alcohol Abuse and Alcoholism, was rampant in Eastern Europe and the Soviet Union. In a study, conducted by Orphan Doctor 1994-1997, 15 out of 1.000 per adoption cases from Russia were afflicted with FASD. That was eight times the worldwide rate. Fetal Alcohol Syndrome is difficult to diagnose before the child is eight months old. It is a non-curable birth defect. 20/20 aired a show "To Russia with love" that dealt with difficult adoptions and brought to public awareness the intense challenges these adoptions bring. Since the Hague Convention on Intercountry

Adoptions in 2008, agencies are now required to disclose the adoptee's background to the future parents. The National Data from 1998 from the Centers for Disease Control and Prevention (CDC) revealed that between 31.9 and 34.5 of women stated that they used alcohol in the three-month period prior to finding out that they were pregnant. In 2000, 4.4 percent of the total births entered in the New Jersey Birth Defect Registry (NJR) meet the eligibility criteria of Fetal Alcohol Spectrum Disorder.

FASD is a reportable birth defect and health care providers are required by New Jersey State law to report FASD to NJ BDR prior to the child turning five. Since 2002, New Jersey has six regional centers for FASD. It is the first in the nation to offer Perinatal Addictions Specialist certification. New Jersey Regional Fetal Alcohol Spectrum Disorder is located at UMDNJ-NJMS. International adoptions are especially popular in Minnesota, which has one of the highest rates of international adoptions in the world (11.3 out of 1,000). In 2003-2004, the International Adoption Clinic at the University of Minnesota screened 483 children of which 79 percent were Russian. Twelve percent of the new cases from the Soviet Union and Eastern Europe were diagnosed with FASD.

CHRONOLOGY

History of Nick's Drug/Alcohol Abuse and
related Criminal activities to date

1996-2005 – Problems in schools with behaviors/learning disabilities – detention and suspensions.

2006 – Juvenile Conference Committee – weapon and possession of pot. On probation-therapy.

11/06 – Arrested – stolen goods - hired private attorney.

2006 – !st Rehab – intensive outpatient program. Started and he refused to attend. Truancy from Special Ed. school for three years on and off, '07 to '09.

2006-2007 – Therapist, Dr. Silver

11/2006 – 10 days in hospital. Adolescent inpatient for suicidal thoughts.

2007 – Questioned by cops for pot in town.

2008 – Arrested – stealing – pot and attorney hired privately. On probation.

2007-2008 – Job at Shoprite. Fired – last 14 months.

2008-2009 – 2nd Rehab – outpatient twice – insurance paid on full.

11/2009 – 3rd Rehab – inpatient and step down to IOP.

6/2010 – Arrested for third-degree felony - assault – private attorney hired – probation for five years.

11/2010 – Department of Labor and Workforce – DR – priority of 1 – "most significantly disabled."

12/2010 – Division of Developmental Disabilities – accepted as client

2011-2012 – Drug Counseling. outpatient.

9/2013 – Arrested for DWI – private attorney hired.

9/2013 – Criminal Justice Advocacy Program involved – case manager appointed.

1/2014 – IDRC and Catholic Charities for alcohol/drug outpatient counseling/testing

3/2013-2/2014 – Worked for one year with assistance of DVR/job coach – fired

3/2014-8/2014 – Collected unemployment benefits.

10/2014 – Discharged from Catholic Charities for Noncompliance/positive drug test.

10/2014 – Arrested for DUI – Second offense.

10/2014 – Detox first time for opiates – eight days.

10/2014 – Transfer to Rehab – stays 30 days.

11/2014 – 3/2015 Lived at ¾ house. Alcoholic poisoning – went to E.R. by ambulance. Progressed to stealing jewelry, cash, debit cards and checks.

3/2015 – 8/2015 – Oxford House – Sober living. Relapse.

8/2015-10/2016 -Detox Florida. Rehabs in Florida.

10/2016- 05/2018- Active addiction

6/2018- Rehab in PA-30 days

7/2018-12/2018-Florida rehab/Partial Hospitalization and IOP

BIBLIOGRAPHY

Delaney, Richard J., and Frank R. Kunstal. *Troubled Transplants: Unconventional Strategies for Helping Disturbed Foster and Adoptive Children.* Wood 'N' Barnes Pub., 1997.

Greene, Ross W. *The Explosive Child: a New Approach for Understanding and Parenting Easily Frustrated, Chronically Inflexible Children.* Harper, 2014.

Hallowell, Edward M., and John J. Ratey. *Driven to Distraction: Recognizing and Coping with Attention Deficit Disorder from Childhood through Adulthood.* Anchor Books, 2011.

Keck, Gregory C., and Regina M. Kupecky. *Adopting the Hurt Child: Hope for Families with Special-Needs Kids.* NavPress, 2009.

Khaleghi, Morteza, and Karen Khaleghi. *The Anatomy of Addiction: Overcoming the Triggers That Stand in the Way of Recovery.* Palgrave Macmillan, 2011.

Magid, Ken, and Carole A. McKelvey. *High Risk: Children without a Conscience*. Bantam Books, 1988.

McKelvey, Carol. *Give Them Roots, Then Let Them Fly:Understanding Attachment Therapy. Give Them Roots, Then Let Them Fly:Understanding Attachment Therapy*, The Attachment Center at Evergreen.

Mitchell, Kathleen. "Partnership for a Drug Free Kids." 2013.

National Organization on Fetal Alcohol Syndrome, www.nofas.org/.

Randolph, Elizabeth. *Children Who Shock and Surprise:A Guide to Attachment Disorders*. 1997.

Streissguth, Ann. *The Challenge of Fetal Alcohol Syndrome: Overcoming Secondary Disabilities*. Univ. of Washington Press, 1997.

Turecki, Stanley. *Difficult Child*. Bantam., 1985.

Welch, Martha G. *Holding Time*. Simon and Schuster, 1989.

Printed in the United States
By Bookmasters